Pacific Prescription: Leukemia Cyclone

poems by

Magdalena Louise Hirt

Finishing Line Press
Georgetown, Kentucky

Pacific Prescription: Leukemia Cyclone

for Ben

ACKNOWLEDGMENTS

I would like to thank my parents for encouraging the bond between my brother and
me. We have had an amazing childhood.

Publisher: Leah Huete de Maines
Editor: Christen Kincaid
Cover Photo: Magdalena Louise Hirt
Author Photo: Magdalena Louise Hirt
Cover Design: Elizabeth Maines McCleavy

Order online: www.finishinglinepress.com
also available on amazon.com

Author inquiries and mail orders:
Finishing Line Press
PO Box 1626
Georgetown, Kentucky 40324
USA

Contents

Water History:
Marquesas to Tuamotu Atolls

Moon with Milk

This moon waits up for me
wanting to talk for hours.
This moon reflects me
to me—I see myself.

Nowhere. Somewhere.

Here. Swaying with Pacific
breeze. This moon tells me
what she wants, where she
will go—if I'm allowed to follow.

A moon with milk. Eclipsed last night.

Now full of light pulling the sea
from underneath me. Leaving
my planets aligned, she chooses
to quietly try to sleep. Her light

on remains, so my thoughts

linger on her like the smell of cookies
in the oven, sugar melting, flavors
blending. A home on the ocean
deep into the world no one sees.

I get her for now, I don't, and won't

share her delicious company
with the boy from the summer,
the girl from Norway, or the dough,
the chocolate chips, or Milky Way.

The Flower Moon

wanes, only allowing the rising
planets—Saturn, Mars, Jupiter,
and Venus enough shine space.
In the night, we talk love stories
before we change shifts—textbook
versus trauma, and the wind
pulls back listening. Full sail—
three bulbed, poled, snapping
full, wind wanting to ease drop a bit
more. My youngest son asks,
May I come back as a boat?
Can I do that? His curious mind
stretching reincarnation. I don't
want to answer, limit, or extend
his existence. I embrace it
to imagine what our boat, *Selkie*,
has seen, has done, has cared for.
I say, maybe, but she's not breathing.
She's not a living thing, yet tonight
I can't swallow those words.
They sit on my tongue needing.
The sails snap again like a sharp
breath, the ocean caresses
the hull, and I ponder her love
story—watching, listening,
holding strong through a squall.

My Window

My window use to be of pine and oak,
a neighborhood corner, singing the song,
"Somewhere Out There" making wishes.

My window then became a look beyond
the corner into stars, singing the song,
"One Love" exhaling smoke into darkness.

My window looked at a back alley,
an all-girl dormitory, singing the song,
"The Beautiful People" experimenting.

My window looked over a river to the city
with babies in my arms, singing the song,
"Whiskey in a Jar" legs kicking, dancing.

My window moved to a glass city, a Victorian,
art flooding the night, dreaming, and singing,
"Skye Boat Song" to move me further.

My window now is framed by a zipper
that opens to the sea, waves that whisper,
wind that whistles, stars that stare, a moon
that hums, clouds that hold their distance,
and I can't help but hear, see, sing, read
the song of water that falls deep into my soul.

Glistening

9849 ft to the bottom of the ocean.
361,603 km to the surface of the moon.
Zoom in. Zoom out. Me. Floating
in between. Fomalhaut, the white star,
marks the mouth of the constellation
of the southern fish, Piscis Austrinus.
It flirts with me from 25 light years away.
The light I see burned when I was 18,
just a month shy of graduating high
school. Cap and gown, I was bound
to a summer of bartending, breaking
rules, skinny dipping in Lake Michigan
waters, surrounded by dunes, land
bound, watching boats come and go.
Glistening now, the ocean reflects
the light back into space, a gentle
transaction like a girl sitting in sand
wondering, like a pile of clothes waiting,
like the moonlight on wet skin shining,
like a mother slipping through the night
reflecting in her eyes deep water history.

In the Blood:
Between the Atolls

Tangled

up in lines holding
bulbed sails like a fish
in a net pulled along
taking in its last breath—
sight of home. The ocean
has me. I won't breathe,
if you take me from her.

Ocean Wind

In the dark, you caress
my thighs, again and again,
completely oblivious
to my unwavering attraction.

Somewhere

I didn't even know existed.

The Tuamotu Atolls—pristine,
shark infested, Pacific Ocean
lagoons that place me painted
in a postcard floating chain
over miniature coral habitats
like a mysterious, hovering,
untouchable constellation.

Ocean Life

like a tough, muffled scream
that has no sound and bites
the shoulder,
                    or a quiet breath
that goes knees deep and floats
out the spine to land in wonder

Bone Marrow:
Tuamotu to Tahiti

Calm

and I just want to scream,
"FREE!" I was not a prisoner.
I was in paradise, but, there,
was I there too long? Sails flap,
breeze tickles, Milky Way, the path.
Here. At sea—I climb on the aft, above
my bed, behind the helm, on the sea
again, I feel the steel in hand pull.

"I'm here. I'm back," I whisper.

"I'll try not to leave too soon,
again. Pause with me
like you did when
the calm stole
you."

Curvish Pull

listen
to her

Moonless

Tuamotu atolls behind
us. Tahiti bound. We leave
rivers of sharks, passes
that pull and push, Remora,
spotted, spawning grouper
that make the coral floor
move, mystery, paradise
in the Pacific. Wing to
wing, the breeze is gentle
as it says goodbye. Blue,
clear water fills my mind.
The trick to floating chain
in my memory. The beach
that gave me tears of joy.
The ocean rocks me,
"It's okay," she says. "Sail."

The Man of the Sea

If he were to step onboard
from the darkness, what

would I say? Would I be
scared, or would I know

his language? Out here.
Nowhere. We could talk.

Above Tahiti

Forty miles out, a squall,
and swells toss us like popcorn.
The sea is entertained, us
a buttery snack on the outskirts
of its South Pacific cyclones.
Everything must be on the floor
sliding this way then that. Motor
on to reach the shadow of Tahiti.
Walls of rain change the color
of sunrise from teeming tangerine
to gray indigo. My jaw tenses.
My hair whips loose batting
my cheeks with snake-morning
tendrils. I'm strapped in, I still
have to hold tight to the helm
as the sea's wet wind gusts
through the cockpit. Tahiti.
Tahiti. Tahiti. A short stretch
away. A yearn for soil, hills,
reefs that stand to the sea.
A wave breaks on port shoving.
Our moving home holds so much
life in a capsule of wood. Breathe.
Tahiti. Tahiti. I whisper it forth
like a sweet and salty spell
that my lips and throat savor.

When

constant
change
becomes
the norm
does stability
and repetition
become
a desire
or
or
or
does that
that movement
become something
of the past
a memory
do you
cling
change
claw
does it slip
between
talons
like water
fall-
ing
ing
Ing

Leukemia Cyclone:
From the States

Leukemia Warriors

House leave, which is a boat leave
for us. The States. Family. Land.
All to accentuate the summer. Then,

my brother gets diagnosed with AML
Leukemia. Leukemia. Leukemia. Denial.
Fear. Grief. Anger. Nothing close to

acceptance. I must be a hero. We must
put sailing on hold, which seems so trivial
now. To sail. To play. To travel. Trivial.

It's time to save my brother's life. Me.
I'm 100%—a bone marrow match.
The donor. Everyone looks to me.

Absolutely, I say. There is nothing more
important than being able to save
his life. Him. For his wife, his son, his

parents, my parents, for me, save him
for me. I can't live in a world where
Uncle Ben doesn't fish, doesn't hunt,

doesn't tell his stories, doesn't laugh.
Bound to the States. Holding onto home,
so he can live, so he can be again.

Leukemia

Leukemia. Leukemia.
LeUkEmIa. leukemia.
leukEmia.
Leu
k
mia. Leukemia. Leu
kemia. LEUKEMIA!
Leu
k
mia.

Finding

Fishing
the purpose that holds
Us still
purposeful

Somewhere
there
A feeder lingers

Bottom strong
such
A scary
bitch

Emotion
can flood
Strength

forgotten
~after reading Transparencies by Meg Bateman

there's a silence in the air
as I take in the group of poems—

the words that linger—
jaws, tentacles, licks, jowls
—and I am swallowed

into a scottish life—
braken, heather, thistle, clover
—have the flowers grown over me
here, land bound, a cure in my blood

have I lost myself in the evergreen
of dunes, the shore of the big pond

jaw raised, can I sing my way out
will the ocean breath me in
—make me interesting again

me—a mother wolf, four cubs
dragged about in my sharp teeth
rolled around by my rough paws

there are no bagpipes on the wind
here—no heather, no thistle
only store-bought blackberries

dè mise dhutsa—what am I to you—
sister, savior, sailor—seasickness,
anxiety turns my stomach—washed up
on the shore, no movement, waves
lap, claw, pull on my waters

the wind moves the trees
—like the soft bark-colored fur
of a squirrel—I'm unseen
scurrying with restlessness

the acorn drops—fall arrives
am I to sink in the sand with worms
or find my blood and bones in deep sea

It Wakes Me

The deep pain in my bones

working on zarxio that will

produce stem cells for my brother

and my story narrows, my voice quiet.

Who will narrate for me?

Who will see my point of view?

Two more tiny pokes in my belly.

The cure for leukemia swims deep.

I become only the picture, framed

by my brother, hung in his house,

my voice remembered, another story

told by his voice. I make the call.

My voice heard one last time

to numb the pain, give my story away.

sibling tree, bend

as my bones set fire and spill
there is hope for more time,
time for mom, for your wife,
for your boys—I build you

a hero in my mind, I guess
I'm a hero to you, my jaw
swollen like a t-rex, mi-
graine constant as bones

make, make, make, spill
stem cells, my skin holding
life like a test tube, picked up
examined, lab-worked, labeled

the air—breathing—is different
to me now, I stare at leaves
moving with wind, or still—
about to explode with color

we are an evergreen together,
leukemia the winter, our needles
not giving into snow's blank color,
becoming the wave that won't

freeze near the shore, you—
for you—I can tell it's hard for you
to look at me—when did that
start—ages ago, or just now

look at me—it hurts—I am here
'the cells will shimmer' mom says
she swims in the pool imagining
she's my cells moving into yours

what will it be like to have my life
back—you to have yours—this time
forward takes a new meaning
wind in a sail, crystal blue water

brother—sister—now more sister,
a giving, donation, a creating,
a changing, a ben-ding like leaves
branch clinging—photosynthesizing

Porcelain Doll

is what my husband refers to me
as when I was on zarxio to spill
stem cells into my blood to cure.
I stare at my husband from across
the island table in the kitchen
of our cottage with a warning
not to come near me—that his love
and care are not allowed to be
accepted—that a tender touch
would send me into a screaming
and thrashing fight for my life.
I move to sit next to the fire
on the couch, and my spine churns
into convulsions—the pain means
it's working. I time, to the minute,
when I can digest more pain meds
to endure the making of this magic—
the heat of it not strengthening
my ceramic material but thinning it
to a delicate, cracked surface
unable to contain what is working
underneath for my brother.

The Pain Subsides,

but thoughts of you don't.

You arrive at dinner, hairless,
a mask, sitting ten feet away
feels like a voyage, a crossing
of vast amounts of water, sails,
winds, storms, calms, adrift
moments, and I still won't reach
you. Your wife is by your side,
and you talk mundane stories,
like usual, barely conversing
on what matters, what I need
to hear, and I feel selfish. My arm
can't reach you, but the bruise
from the donation is tender
to remind me that my stem cells
will reach the important part
of you to cure your leukemia.
You make another joke—something
meaningless. There is laughter.
It cures, but I can't get my eyes
to tell you what I need to hear—
your fears, your pain, your thoughts,
your love, your troubles, your mind—
I must be selfish to want to hear
what matters. You make another
joke. We laugh. The yard we sit
in is as separate as hospital rooms—
tidy, clean, sound clamped down
keeping our doors unlocked but shut.

FU 🤍 ✕ Leukemia

You post us as a duo, teenage years,
and my plane lifts off to Tahiti—back
to *Selkie*, we go. We were standing
in your first truck—rusty, coon tail
included. We. Could conquer. Life.
Now. Leukemia. Like the rust eats
the truck, we eat the cancer away
—restart the blood—restart …
what confusingly interrupted *our
lives*. Your wife's, my sister's, eyes
tear. It seems, we, are more worried
for her than *us*. Yes. That's right.
That's good. That's the distraction,
we need. The truck rumbles on. *Our*
teenage selves buckle up—nothing
like safety in *this* disintegrating
false bubble of casement that will
happily lie to us convincingly. *Snap*.
Buckled in. The ongoing forest
stands waiting contemplation.

The Cure:
Back in Tahiti

Back to. Tahiti.

I don't think a poetic zen can be reached
after 47 hours of travel and an 11-hour school day.

The sun begins to set and beams through the rental
in an unreal horizontal way. I find a segment of the floor

to hide from the vitamin D. The horizon is vast
again... miles reach like tendrils of illusions.

Roosters crow or do they howl? Speaking to each
other from multiple sides of high-risen earth.

Push me in the dirt. I still need recouping.

the bruise

on my arm dissipates to a heart shape in Tahiti

there is only memory of the bone marrow donation here

the waiting for my brother's treatment, for the transplant

it was his birthday yesterday, my parents' anniversary

from afar I ask him to hold strong, wait for my magic

he shares his birthday with jean-claude van damme

we compare them, my brother claiming the name

big sweetie—for that's what he is—a big sweetie

muscles and tattoos with a tender heart turns 46

leukemia blasts unseen—how do we, him and I,

become action heroes in our own stories

my kids ask if the bruise will ever go away

a fellow sailor sees it and is taken aback

wanting to know more, a tumor lingers

in him, he needs saving, the dogs,

the roosters, the bats, go silent

in this night in Tahiti while

my skin repairs

blood

Water Again:
A Stop in Moorea

The Stars Again.
    ~double wishing

Cold of the steel boom hugged
In my arms as we stare into ether.

Home.

Music spills like the tropical flowers
That float—giving us room to anchor.

Breathe.

It wasn't too far from a few choices.
Just like two falling stars. We aligned.

Home.

Hug of cold steel and rough line for me.
A new island, new bay, that anchors us.

Successful.

Pondering

One artist to another—
One milky light to another
that spills moon over water—
This light—Drums and paints—
This light slops big strokes,
darts, disappears, and reappears,
Rippling—It makes my body
Dance. Disappear. Reappear.
I shake—starless in a crevice
of mountain—Drums in my bones
Knock knock. Beat. Beat. Thrum.
Stop.

A voice
Barks—
My daughter
Waits.

Yet.
A beat.
The beat.
Has my body.
The light—electric
on the water. Me.
Moving—it thrums
through me. I ripple.
Like the sea
Hovering
Living
In the movement
of night off the bow.

Calming Wind:
Moorea to Bora Bora

Transplant

Leukemia—a memory like starlight
in space. My stem cells replace,
reboot, regrow to give the power
that burns new fight. The moon
eclipses and gives your blood
the magic myths are made from.
Bags hang, tubes stretch, your wife
by your side, my shimmer in veins.
Like the dark side of the moon,
leukemia is a memory. The bright,
full side filled with mountains,
craters, new stories to tell. New
poems to write like space needs
purpose, like starlight needs eyes.

And it's me again

Orion. Fairy bioluminescent dust. Wind.
Slipping through the Otherworld. Noticed.

But allowed. Sails capture the whispers
of the selkies, sea dragons, and zodiacs.

She's been waiting patiently for me,
the water, crashing when I wept, stilling

when I slept. A river flows behind my wake,
leukemia conquered. The river leaves

a trail on the ocean like the trail left
imprinted in my blood. Just a trail. No need

to tread the twists and turns again. Let
the trail overgrow with seaweed, whale

migrations, and turtle searches. Let
the life in Pacific completely muddle up

the interruption. The wind hits my tied up
hair. I am a warrior. Home—in my element.

www.ingramcontent.com/pod-product-compliance
Lightning Source LLC
Chambersburg PA
CBHW020221090426
42734CB00008B/1159